The Tre

*cheual
conditinated*

Clean

MAY

Seniors'

Jokes

Look for the other books in
The Treasury of Clean Jokes series:

the treasury of

Clean
Seniors'
Jokes

TAL D. BONHAM
& JACK GULLEDGE

BROADMAN
&HOLMAN
PUBLISHERS

Nashville, Tennessee

© 1997 by Tal D. Bonham
All rights reserved
Printed in the United States of America

4263-65
0-8054-6365-8

Published by Broadman & Holman Publishers,
Nashville, Tennessee
Acquisitions and Development Editor: Janis Whipple
Page Design: Desktop Miracles, Inc., Addison, Texas

Dewey Decimal Classification: 808.87
Subject Heading:
JOKES—COLLECTED / ELDERLY
Library of Congress Card Catalog Number: 96-53375

**Library of Congress
Cataloging-in-Publication Data**
Bonham, Tal D., 1934–91.
　　　The treasury of clean seniors' jokes / Tal D.
　　Bonham, Jack Gulledge. — 2nd. ed.
　　　　　p.　cm.
　　　Rev. ed. of: The treasury of clean senior adults'
jokes.　1989.
　　　ISBN 0-8054-6365-8 (pbk.)
　　　1. Aging—Humor.　2. Old age—Humor.
　　3. Aged—Humor.　I. Gulledge, Jack, 1924– .
　　II. Bonham, Tal D., 1934–91. The treasury of
　　clean senior adult jokes.　III. Title.
　　PN6231.A43B66　　1997
　　818'.5402—dc21
　　　　　　　　　　　　　96-53375
　　　　　　　　　　　　　CIP

97 98 99 00 01 1 2 3 4 5

Dedication

In 1991, Tal Bonham passed away,
leaving a legacy of both love and humor
to his family and friends,
and a legacy of laughter to all his readers.
In revising
The Treasury of Clean Seniors' Jokes,
the publisher asked his wife
for a new dedication written
in memory of Tal D. Bonham.

In the past five years, since my husband's
heavenly homecoming,
his humor has enabled me,
my family, and those who loved him,
to cope with his loss.
Our four children agreed, at the time of
selecting
the Scripture inscription on his tombstone,
that the following would be appropriate—

"A merry heart doeth good like a medicine"
(Prov. 17:22).
—Faye Bonham

Dedication

From Faye and Tal to Our Moms—

Esther Trowbridge in Neosho, Missouri,
Lee Cravey in Tuscaloosa, Alabama, and
Maggie Wright in Bessemer, Alabama

Writing itself is a lot of laughs. And for those of us lucky enough to make a living at it, it's double the fun. For these years of journalistic joy, I owe a special debt of gratitude to two people, Erwin McDonald and Ernest Mosley.

Erwin, long-time editor of *The Arkansas Baptist Newsmagazine,* not only published my first manuscript in the early 1950s, but tutored me by mail.

In the early 1970s Ernest, who at the time was a supervisor at the Baptist Sunday School Board, gave me my first editor's job.

To my dear friends and fellow scribes, Erwin and Ernest, I dedicate these fun pages.
—Jack Gulledge

Contents

Introduction

What do you call a book aimed primarily at senior adults? I realize that some people don't like to be called "senior adults." One famous journalist said, "The next person who calls me a senior citizen, I'm going to call him a 'junior citizen.'" A psychologist friend of mine said, "Maybe it doesn't really matter what they call us as long as they smile when they say it."

Well, we're smiling when we say —here's a joke book designed primarily for senior adults. We hope you enjoy it. We've tried to put it together from the biblical perspective that, "A merry heart doeth good like a medicine" (Prov. 17:22). We hope this little book will be good medicine for you and those with whom you share its humor.

—Tal D. Bonham

The person who laughs—*lasts!*

No age group enjoys a lasting laugh more than senior adults. It's God's medicine of mirth for difficult times. Someone once likened humor to shock absorbers that help weary pilgrims over the rough roads of daily struggle. Truly a hearty laugh is like a healing ray of hope in a sickroom of despair. So put on a happy face. "Against the assault of laughter," Mark Twain said, "nothing can stand."

Within these pages you'll find our attempt to pass along a healthy dose of mirth. A few of the stories, collected over many years from forgotten sources, are true; others are not. But they're all designed to help senior adults enjoy the lighter side of life. After all, we can't take life too seriously—we're never going to get out of it alive anyway!

So sit back. Grin. Turn on the old tickle box. Let the medicine of mirth heal the soul and keep life in perspective.

Repeat daily the prayer of Chester Cathedral:

Give me a sense of humor, Lord;
Give me the grace to see a joke,
To get some happiness from life,
And pass it on to other folk.

—Jack Gulledge

You Know You're about to Become a Senior Adult When...

You don't care where your wife goes as long as you don't have to go with her.

You get short of breath opening the telephone directory.

The grandkids come home and tell you what they are studying in history, and you remember studying the same subjects in current-events class.

You become exhausted simply by wrestling with your conscience.

You decide procrastination is the best approach to life, but you never get around to it.

You look forward to a dull evening.

You walk with your head held high because you're trying to get used to your bifocals.

You sit in a rocking chair and you can't get it going.

Your knees buckle, but your belt won't.

Dialing long distance wears you out.

"Burning the midnight oil" means staying up past 9 P.M.

Your back goes out more than you do.

You sink your teeth into a steak and they stay there.

You bend over to tie your shoes and look around to see if there's something else you can do while you're down there.

Accidents

I still get nervous when I speak after all these years. It goes with being a minister. It all started about forty years ago when I performed my first wedding. I did OK until I pronounced the couple husband and wife. I waited for the groom to kiss the bride, but he just stood there. Then in a nervous high-pitched tone I blurted out, "It's kisstomary to cuss the bride!"

And he probably has ever since!

The car skidded to an abrupt stop. The first person on the scene screamed, "Look at that awful sight splattered all over the inside of the windshield!"

"Are you badly hurt?" they asked the man in the front seat.

"Nah," the driver replied, "but this pizza is a mess!"

"What should I take, Doctor," gasped the tense patient, "when I'm run down?"

"Try the license number first," replied the bored doctor, "then get the make of the car!"

A telephone directory in a large city accidentally got this ad mixed in with the listing of funeral directors:

"When away, keep in touch by long distance. Phone ahead for reservations. Let them know you're on the way!"

An obituary notice in a newspaper recounted the impressive rites of a funeral service and then noted: "A spectator slipped at the gravesite and broke his leg. The accident cast a cloud of gloom over the whole occasion."

A man came in to the doctor's office, and the receptionist asked him what he had. "Shingles," he answered.

She took his name, address, medical insurance information, and told him to take a seat. Fifteen minutes later another nurse came in and weighed him, took his temperature, and told him to go into the examining room and take off his clothes.

Thirty minutes later the doctor came in and asked him what he had. Again he answered, "Shingles."

"Where?" the doctor probed.

"Outside in the truck," the bewildered man responded. "Where do you want me to unload them?"

"How in the world did you happen to hit that other car?" asked the policeman investigating the accident.

"It was my wife's fault," the man replied. "She fell asleep in the back seat!"

Advice

I like to drive, but one day I had a frightening experience. I was out in the country when my car broke down. I got out to take a look under the hood.

Just then an old horse trotted by, said, "Better check the gasoline," and galloped on down the road. I was so frightened I ran to a nearby farmhouse and told the farmer what had happened.

"Was it an old horse with a floppy ear?" he asked.

"Yes! Yes!" I replied.

"Well then," the farmer drawled, "don't pay no attention to him. He don't know nothin' about cars."

A doctor questioned his patient, "It's strange you haven't been to see me in years. What other doctors have you been seeing?"

"No doctors," replied the patient, "only my pharmacist."

"Why, goodness, man!" bellowed the doctor, "Are you in your right mind? That druggist isn't medically qualified. You certainly shouldn't listen to him. What crazy and idiotic thing did he tell you?"

"He told me to come see you!" answered the patient.

The young bachelor was discussing his marital status with his grandfather. "I've dated several women and come close to marriage several times. However," he said, "I just haven't been able to find the wife for me."

The grandfather remarked, "You're going to find yourself left out in the cold some day without a wife."

"Aw," said the young bachelor, "there are plenty of fish left in the sea!"

"Yes," pondered the grandfather. "Just remember that after a while the bait is not what it used to be!"

Aging

My wife bought a new line of expensive cosmetics guaranteed to make her look years younger. After a lengthy sitting before the mirror applying the "miracle" products she asked, "Darling, honestly what age would you say I am?"

Looking her over carefully, I replied, "Judging from your skin, twenty; your hair, eighteen; and your figure, twenty-five."

"Oh, you flatterer!" she gushed.

"Hey, wait a minute!" I interrupted. "I haven't added them up yet."

Growing older is merely a matter of feeling your corns rather than feeling your oats.

A devout Christian was taking the aging process a little hard. As he noticed the wrinkles, loose skin, receding gums, and arthritis, his response was, "I'm not going to say that God made a mistake when He created old age but I'll tell you one thing: when I get to heaven I'm going to talk to Him about it."

An Old-Timer: one who can remember when a "bureau" was a piece of furniture.

"Now, Mrs. Lyons," said the doctor. "You say you have shooting pains in the neck, dizziness, and constant nausea. Just for the record, how old are you?"

"I'm going to be thirty-nine on my next birthday," replied the woman.

"Hmmmmm," muttered the doctor. "Got a slight loss of memory too!"

Trim Figures: what some people do when they tell their age.

QUESTION: How is life like a taxi cab?
ANSWER: The meter keeps going whether you're going somewhere or just standing still.

Children: a great comfort in old age, and often that which helps you get there sooner.

I have to admit to aging because:

Now that I know my way around, I don't feel like going.

My forehead is getting higher and my energy lower.

My wife powders and I puff.

It takes me longer to rest than it does to get tired.

I'm at the stage where my passion has turned to pensions.

Senior Adult: Reaching the age where you've got to prove that you are just as good as you never were.

WIFE: "Well, you really know how to flatter a woman. That was a stroke of genius when you told Mrs. Jones that she didn't look a day older than her daughter."

HUSBAND: "Yeah, did you see the look on her face when I said that?"

WIFE: "No, I didn't notice. I was too busy watching the expression on her daughter's face!"

A sign posted at a retirement village: "Lord, keep me alive while I'm still living."

The five *B*s of old age: balding, bursitis, bifocals, bulges, and bunions.

Old age is when Father Time catches up with Mother Nature.

It's a time when a person gets exhausted just wrestling with his conscience.

It's a time when our narrow waists and broad minds change places.

It's a time when the sight of a big, round

harvest moon reminds us to have the furnace checked.

It's a time when boys consider women charmless, and girls consider men harmless.

It's a time of life when we shun those crowded gatherings where people outnumber the comfortable chairs.

Arguments

"You're more than seventy-five years old, slim and trim, and have a tremendous tan. What's the secret of your success?" asked the doctor.

"Well," he explained, "my wife and I have been married for more than fifty years. Before we got married we agreed that if I ever lost my temper I was to say nothing."

"That sounds good," said the doctor. "What kind of arrangement did your wife make in case she lost her temper?"

"We agreed that if she ever lost her temper I would simply go outside. That's where my good health comes in. I've spent most of my life outdoors."

One couple lived together for sixty years without a single argument. Their secret? They shared the same hearing aid!

A man and his wife were eating in a restaurant in Canton, Ohio. They were having an argument on how to pronounce *Canton*. He said the emphasis was on the first syllable, while she said it was on the second.

He called a high school student who worked in the restaurant over to their table and asked, "Please, very slowly, tell us where we are."

The high school student stepped back, looked at the couple, and said very slowly, "Bur . . . ger . . . King!"

An older minister was advising a younger minister. "You will discover," he said, "that in nearly every group there is at least one person who will want to argue with you."

"What shall I do?" queried the young minister.

"Well," the senior adult replied, "your first impression will be to cut him off or put him down; however, I advise you to think very carefully before doing that. He is probably the only one who is listening."

Baldness

QUESTION: What is a bald man's greatest wish?
ANSWER: Dandruff.

SENIOR ADULT: "I take great comfort in the fact that they don't put marble tops on cheap tables."
JUNIOR ADULT: "Unfortunately, they are found primarily on antiques."

The older a man gets, the more ways he learns to part his hair. Some men pull what little bit of hair they have around on their head to cover their baldness. However, as a man gets even older, he realizes there are basically only three ways to wear your hair—parted, unparted, and departed.

Bulges

If you think old soldiers just fade away, try getting into your old uniform.

When you allow yourself to gain too much weight, but you want to appear as though you really don't care, just say this to your friends: "I'd rather plump up than dry up!"

You know, doctors say if we eat slower we will eat less. Big deal! We all learned that during the Depression as members of large families.

The Public Health Service reports that there are at least five million overweight people in the United States—that's in round figures, of course.

The pleasures of eating are fleeting. But the pleasures of fasting are lasting.

There's one thing that will give you more for your money than it did ten years ago—the penny scale at the corner drugstore.

If at first you don't recede, diet, diet again.

The best place for your bathroom scale is in front of your refrigerator.

A sign in a reducing salon read: "Please Do Not Feed The Customers."

Diets are for persons who are thick and tired of it all.

A diet is what you keep putting off while you keep putting on.

Two kids were examining a bathroom scale. "What's it for?" one asked.

"I don't know," the other answered. "I think you stand on it and it makes you mad."

Dieting is slowing down to make a curve.

"What do you think of Medicare?" someone asked a backwoods woman.

"Oh, I like it a lot," she replied. "I took it for a month and lost ten pounds."

Church and Ministers

A pastor finished a glowing message one Sunday morning. A stately grandmother with her young grandson shook the pastor's hand at the back door and announced, "Oh, Pastor, I'm just filled with your message!"

The pastor, quite embarrassed with such a response, turned to the little boy and asked, "Well, young man, what did you think of the sermon?"

The little boy looked up at the pastor and said, "To be honest, Pastor, I got a belly full of you too!"

The only time the pastor ever sees some people is when they're hatched, matched, or dispatched!

I took my small grandson to church. He watched as the choir came out of the side door in white robes and took their places.

Then he leaned over to me and whispered, "Look, Granddaddy! They're all going to get a haircut."

Old Granny was eighty-seven, and her health was very poor; but she definitely would not consent to see a doctor. Finally her grand-daughter asked the family physician to come to the house and examine her grandmother thoroughly.

After the doctor had taken his leave, Granny yelled for her granddaughter.

"Betty," she said, "who in the world was that nice young preacher?"

"Well, I have to confess, Granny," said the granddaughter, "that was no preacher—he was a doctor."

"A doctor!" exclaimed the grandmother with great disappointment. "Well, I thought he looked a little too familiar to be a preacher!"

One preacher said he knows that when the resurrection takes place his church members will beat all others out of the grave because the Bible says: "The dead in Christ shall rise first."

Church typewriters are notorious for making embarrassing blunders in church bulletins. Intending to use *take*, one pastor's column read: "Many calls come to the church each week and we conscientiously *fake* an interest in every one of them."

I pastored in a small town of about twelve hundred folks after graduating from seminary, and I had a lot of stored-up knowledge to dispose of. On the Sunday before the Fourth of July, I preached a rip-roaring sermon with strong patriotic overtones.

Several people joined the church that morning. My six-year-old son went down the line of new members, shaking their hands vigorously and saying, "God bless you in the name of the United States of America!"

My sweet little wife suggested that when I prepare a sermon I should remember the advertisement of a new washing machine: "After it spins dry, it shuts itself off automatically."

The Sunday School teacher explained to the little boys in the class that "Lot was warned to take his wife and flee from the city, but his wife turned to salt."

"What happened to the flea?" one little boy asked.

Once while I was preaching, a man in the back row shouted, "I can't hear you!"

Another man seated down front got up and shouted back, "I can! Come up here and I'll gladly change places with you!"

Confusion

Psychologist: A man who tells you something you already know in words that you can't understand.

The following are actual excuses submitted by parents in one northeastern Pennsylvania school district:

"Dear School: Please ackuse [sic] John for being absent January 28, 29, 30, 31, 32, 33."

"I kept Billy home because she had to go Christmas shopping because I didn't know what size she wears."

"My son is under the doctor's care and should not take P.E. Please execute [sic] him."

"Please excuse Joyce from P.E. for a few days. Yesterday she fell out of a tree and misplaced her hip."

"Please excuse Jimmy from being. It was his father's fault."

A doctor, writing in the usual scribbled fashion, gave a prescription to one of his patients. The patient put it in his pocket and forgot to have it filled.

Two years later he pulled it out of his pocket, showed it to a bus driver, and received a free ride to a neighboring city. He decided to press his luck and was allowed to enter an art museum, several movies, and a Broadway musical.

He flashed it a time or two at restaurants and received a 20 percent discount on his meals. One day his granddaughter happened to pick it up and play it on the piano, and she won a scholarship to the conservatory of music.

From the California Newspaper Publishers Association, here is an example of a typographical error in the classified section of a small-town newspaper, and the subsequent disastrous attempts to correct it:

(Monday) "FOR SALE—R. D. Jones has one sewing machine for sale. Phone 948–0707 after 7 p.m. and ask for Mrs. Kelly who lives with him cheap."

(Tuesday) "NOTICE—We regret having erred in R. D. Jones's ad yesterday. It should have read: 'One sewing machine for sale. Cheap. Phone 948-0707 and ask for Mrs. Kelly who lives with him after 7 p.m.'"

(Wednesday) "NOTICE—R. D. Jones has informed us that he has received several annoying telephone calls because of the error we made in his classified ad yesterday. His ad stands correct as follows: 'FOR SALE—R. D. Jones has one sewing machine for sale. Cheap.

Phone 948-0707 p.m. and ask for Mrs. Kelly who loves with him.'"

(Thursday) "NOTICE—I, R. D. Jones, have no sewing machine for sale. I smashed it. Don't call 948-0707, as the telephone has been out. I have not been carrying on with Mrs. Kelly. Until yesterday she was my house-keeper, but she quit.'"

A cowboy said to a city slicker, "Hey, fellow, you're getting your saddle on backwards, aren't you?"

"That's what you think," the city dude replied. "You don't know which way I'm going."

One day two men, clad in hospital gowns, sat in the office of an emergency room. "I only wanted to have my eyes examined," complained one.

"You're lucky," replied the other. "I just came in to read the meter!"

The doctor grabbed his coat and hat and started out the front door. "I've got to go," he explained to his teenage daughter. "Some man on the phone just said he couldn't live without me!"

"Just a minute, Dad!" she replied. "I believe that call was for me."

Courting

They had just celebrated their fiftieth anniversary. As they were driving across town to their home, she remarked, "You know, we used to sit closer to each other in the car in our courting days over fifty years ago."

"I haven't moved!" he exclaimed.

On their sixtieth wedding anniversary, a reporter came to interview them. "What big problems have you had in your marriage?" he asked the elderly woman.

"Well, there's really been only two—Pa and the fire."

"What do you mean, 'Pa and the fire'?" asked the reporter.

With a gleam in her eye, she explained, "When I paid too much attention to one, the other went out!"

My grandson wanted to know if I could remember my first kiss.

"Son," I replied, "I can't even remember my last one!"

An elderly woman was telling her daughter about a date with a ninety-year-old man.

"Would you believe, I had to slap his face three times."

"Do you mean," the daughter asked in disgust, "that old man got fresh with you?"

"Oh, no!" her mother explained, "I had to keep slapping his face to keep him awake."

> *Oh, the innocent victims of Cupid,*
> *Remember this terse little verse:*
> *"To let a fool kiss you is stupid,*
> *To let a kiss fool you is worse."*

Just remember, kissing is a do-it-yourself job. Don't be like the man who hadn't kissed his wife in twenty years—but shot the man who did!

In her later years the famous actress Sarah Bernhardt lived in an apartment high over Paris. An old admirer climbed all the stairs to see her one day. He asked her breathlessly, "Why do you live so high up?"

"Dear friend," she replied, "it is the only way I can still make the hearts of men beat faster."

Death

MAN: "Can I come over later today to make arrangements for my wife's funeral service?"

FUNERAL DIRECTOR: "Your wife? Didn't we bury her three years ago?"

MAN: "Yeah, we did; however, I married again."

FUNERAL DIRECTOR: "Well, congratulations!"

It's not good for your health to think of yourself too much. You might die laughing.

ZEB: "I didn't know that your son was a funeral director. I thought you said he was a doctor."

ZEKE: "Well, no, I only told you that he followed the medical profession!"

Family: One who prevents you from dying a natural death.

Pathologist: The one who tells your family what you were being cured of when you died.

Consultant: Another doctor who is called in at the last minute to share the blame.

"Now, Rachel," the doctor informed his patient, "there is absolutely no doubt that you will fully recover."

"But why are you so sure?" replied Rachel. "You said before that this was an extremely serious disease with the odds against me!"

"Quite right," replied the doctor. "My medical guidebook clearly states that eleven out of every twelve patients with your illness succumb to it."

"This doesn't reassure me, Doctor," replied Rachel shakily.

"Well, it should," answered the physician. "You see, you are the twelfth patient I've treated with this disease—and the first eleven died!"

An old, grumpy doctor with a none-too-good reputation died, oddly enough, in poverty.

His few friends decided to solicit donations for the burial and proceeded to ask several of his patients. Unfortunately, the first one they asked was an old man equally as disagreeable as the doctor and who had no liking for the medical profession.

"What have you scavengers put me down for?" scowled the old man.

"Ten dollars is what we would like," quickly replied one of them.

The old man took out his checkbook, wrote a check for $120, and added sarcastically, "Now, go get busy and bury a dozen of them!"

A young upstart insurance salesman was trying to sell a ninety-five-year-old man an insurance policy. "No, I'm not interested," said the kindly old gentleman. "I don't plan to live that long."

"Well," said the insurance salesman, "we have a special today on a ten-year insurance policy."

"No," the old man said, "I don't plan to live that long."

"Well, sir, it is my privilege to inform you that my company has just issued a brand new five-year policy and you'll be the first one to receive this offer."

The ninety-five-year-old man smiled and said calmly, "Look, young man, you don't seem to understand. At my age I don't even buy green bananas!"

SEVENTY-FIVE-YEAR-OLD MAN: "When I die I hope it is in a hurry. I'd be satisfied to die in the crash of a speeding car."
EIGHTY-FIVE-YEAR-OLD MAN: "I think it would be better to die in a plane crash."

NINETY-FIVE-YEAR-OLD MAN: "I've got a better idea than either of you—I'd rather die from smoke inhalation from blowing out one hundred candles on my birthday cake."

"Grandma, what happens when we die?"

"Well," his grandma explained, "God forms us from the dust and we are born. When we die, our bodies turn back to dust."

Later that day her grandson found a pile of dirt under the bed. He ran screaming, "Grandma! Come quick! Somebody's under the bed either coming or going."

A gentleman was getting a little nervous after a three-doctor bedside conference. The nurse had to ask one of the doctors to return.

"Do calm yourself down," soothed the doctor. "Why have you gotten so excited?"

"Well, it was all that arguing by you three doctors as to what was wrong with me. You all must not know what is wrong with me, and I'm worried," answered the patient.

"Oh, don't pay any attention to those other doctors," replied the physician. "They don't know—but I do, and I am positive the autopsy will prove me correct!"

Definitions

Parking Space: An area which disappears as you are making a U-turn.

Highbrow: A person educated beyond their intelligence.

Social Grace: When you start out on the right foot rather than putting it in your mouth.

Charity: That generous impulse to give away something you have no use for.

Conceit: A form of "I" strain.

Flattery: The art of telling a person exactly what he thinks of himself.

Proverb: A short sentence based on long experience.

Laziness: The habit of resting before you get tired.

Parking Meter: A piggy bank on a hitching post.

Prejudice: Weighing the facts with your thumb on the scale.

Social Tact: Making people feel at home when you wish they were.

Poise: The ability to keep talking while the other person picks up the check.

Small Town: A place where it's no sooner done than said.

Committee: A group that keeps minutes and wastes hours.

Childhood: That happy period when nightmares occur only during sleep.

Egotism: The art of seeing qualities in yourself which others can't see.

Girdle: An ingenious device invented to keep an unfortunate situation from spreading.

Egotist: A person who thinks if he hadn't been born, people would wonder why.

Prune: A plum that has seen better days.

Doctors

The three stages of being sick: ill, pill, bill.

"That pain in your leg is caused by old age," the doctor told his elderly patient.

"That can't be," said the man. "The other leg is the same age and it doesn't hurt a bit."

Doctor's Receptionist: One who methodically arranges patients' appointments so that the maximum amount of contagious diseases may be transferred in the waiting room to the maximum number of patients in a minimum amount of time.

"Oh, I had a pitiful case today," Dr. Hack informed his wife. "One of the patients died after he drank a quart of varnish."

"What a horrible end," replied his wife.

"A horrible end, yes," said the doctor, "but a glossy finish!"

I know a doctor who will not operate unless it is absolutely necessary—unless he absolutely needs the money.

"Now, John," said the psychiatrist, "you've been seeing me for months, and you seem to be getting worse. What is your problem?"

"It's this terrible feeling of not belonging," cried the patient. "Since paying all your bills, my house doesn't belong to me, my car doesn't belong to me, my . . .!"

During the peak of the cold and virus season last winter, my doctor was giving a lot of penicillin shots. Tacked to the door of his office was a sign that read; "To Save Time, Please Back into the Office."

After quite a bout, my doctor said, "You've been a very sick man. In fact, it was your strong constitution that pulled you through."

"That's good to know," I replied. "I trust you will keep that in mind when you make out my bill."

Do you know what a specialist is? He's a doctor who has his patients trained to become ill only during office hours.

Driving

It takes hundreds of nuts to hold a car together but only one to scatter it all over the highway.

Somebody asked me how long it took for my wife to learn to drive. "Come this fall," I replied, "it will be three years."

I remember teaching her to drive. "Go on green," I explained, "stop on red, and take it easy when my face turns white."

Just kidding. My wife is just as good a driver as I am—and she can do it on either side of the road.

She's really careful and always looks both ways before going through a red light. I wouldn't say she has had a lot of accidents, but I call her car "The Bullet"—it's all shot!

But she's prepared for an emergency. That's why she always drives with the emergency brake on.

Once on a trip while she was driving, the brakes failed going down a steep grade. "I can't stop!" she screamed. "What shall I do?"

"Brace yourself, darling," I shouted, "and hit something cheap."

Once the taillight of her car went out, but she got it fixed. She stopped at a service station and had the man add a quart of red oil.

One day a policeman stopped her and said, "Lady, you were traveling sixty miles an hour."

"It's not possible," she insisted, "I've only been driving twenty minutes."

The other day she put a penny in a parking meter and bent down to take a look. "Oh my goodness!" she exclaimed, "I've lost one hundred pounds!"

One day I was driving. My wife was sitting beside me and my mother-in-law was in the back seat. Both were giving me instructions. Finally, I had had enough. I stopped the car and said to my wife, "Now, I want to know who is driving this car? You or your mother?"

Actually, the wife who drives from the back-seat of a car is no worse than the husband who cooks from the dining room table.

Most accidents are caused by motorists who drive in high while their minds are in neutral.

Have you ever noticed that the only time a car's windshield wiper works perfectly is when it's holding a parking ticket?

Eating

Food prices are going up so fast that it's soon going to be cheaper to eat the money.

Isn't it too bad we don't retain as much of what we read as what we eat?

My wife makes good enthusiastic stew—she puts everything she has into it.

And you ought to taste her Lucifer cake. It was supposed to be angel food cake, but it fell.

She's thoughtful too. She sets my plate before me and says, "There you are, darling. It's cooked just the way you'd better like it!"

I'm not saying her cooking is bad, but penciled on the wall of our kitchen are the words: "Duncan Hines wept here!"

Every evening when I get home I greet my wife with a kiss and say, "Hi, honey, what's thawing?"

I complained to my wife, "Where does all that grocery money go?"

"Stand sideways and look in the mirror," she replied.

I'll give her credit. She knows how to serve company. She can fix food either way—so they'll come back or so they won't.

There's a new Chinese restaurant for dieters. They serve all the food you can eat for fifty cents. Trouble is—they only give you one chopstick.

Adam and Eve had the only perfect marriage. That was because he didn't have to hear about all the men she could have married, and she didn't have to hear about the way his mother cooked!

What keeps most would-be investors out of the stock market is the supermarket.

Epitaphs

Epitaph on a hypochondriac's grave: "I Told You I Was Sick."

A California lawyer's gravestone read: "Final Decree."

A henpecked Illinois lawyer listed the names of his three wives, then proclaimed: "The Defense Rests."

A newsman's epitaph said: "Copy All In."

An Iowa traveling salesman ordered: "My Trip Is Ended. Send My Samples Home."

The family of a railroad man carved this question on his stone: "Papa, Did You Wind Your Watch?"

An Indiana teacher had a brief memorial: "School Is Out. Teacher Has Gone Home."

An avid baseball fan said it in two words: "Play Ball!"

Exercise

He was in good shape even though he was ninety years of age. Knowing that he was a former body-builder and great athlete, a newspaper reporter asked, "What exercise do you do to stay fit?"

"My boy," replied the old man, "when you're pushing ninety, that's the only exercise you need!"

A reporter was interviewing a man on his ninety-ninth birthday. "I certainly hope I can come back next year and see you reach the century mark," he said.

"Can't see any reason why not, young feller," the old-timer replied. "You look healthy enough to me!"

They had lived together in the same house for over fifty years. It had been their custom to take an evening walk every day in a open field behind their house.

One evening, they came to a little creek that ran across the open field. "Do you remember how I used to jump that creek flat-footed?"

"Yes," she said, "but that was when we were younger."

"I can still do it," he exclaimed.

Before she could stop him, he took his stance on one side of the creek, squatted down, and leaped forward. Both feet landed squarely in the middle of the creek.

As he waded out of the muddy creek and started back to the house, he commented to his wife, "That's strange! I guess I just didn't notice that creek getting wider through the years."

"You're looking well," said a friend to a ninety-five-year-old former athlete who had kept himself in good shape through the years.

"It's not my appearance that bothers me these days," said the old man, "it's my disappearance!"

False Teeth

A little girl was fascinated by her grandfather taking out his false teeth and brushing them, so she asked him to do it again. She stood there amazed, then demanded, "Now, take off your nose!"

Reflecting on their marriage of over fifty years, he was sitting in his recliner and she was sitting in hers.

"You know," she said, "things have really changed since our marriage."

"How's that?" he asked.

"Well," she said, "you used to sit very close to me instead of in a separate chair."

"Well, I can remedy that," he said as he got up and moved over to one end of the couch.

As she sat on the other end of the couch, she complained, "You used to sit closer to me than this."

"Well," he said, I can remedy that too," as he moved over close to her.

"You used to put your arm around my shoulders."

"How's that?" he asked, as he put his arm up on the back of the couch.

"Do you remember you used to lean over and nudge my neck with your nose?"

As he nudged her neck with his nose she had one more complaint, "Darling, don't you remember you used to nibble on my earlobes?"

Quickly, he jumped up and left the room. *Oh my,* she thought to herself, *I've hurt his feelings.*

"Where are you going?" she cried.

"To get my teeth!"

Don't ask me if my cold teeth chatter.
We don't sleep together so it doesn't matter.

The theater usher quickly dispatched himself down front where a man was crawling around on his hands and knees. "Sir," he said, "you're disturbing several people around you. What's the problem?"

"I've lost my gum!" said the man as he continued to prowl around the seats.

"Sir," the usher said, "if that's your only problem, let me offer you another stick of gum so you can sit down and watch the movie. One stick of gum is not worth all this disturbance."

"But I'm afraid you don't understand," explained the man, "My false teeth are in that gum!"

Farming

My cousin lived on a small farm. They called it "Oleo Acres"—it was one of the cheaper spreads.

They raised hogs instead of corn and potatoes. "Because," my cousin explained, "hogs don't take no hoein'."

Once I visited my country cousin and helped with the milking. I must have done well. I got milk out of three spigots.

I guess I was ignorant of country life. I pointed and asked my cousin why that cow didn't have horns. "Well, there are several reasons," he explained. "Some cows don't have horns until later in life. Others have them removed. And still others are born without them. But this one doesn't have any horns because it's a horse."

One afternoon I climbed a fence into a pasture and saw a vicious-looking bull.

"Hey!" I called to my cousin. "Is this bull safe?"

"Yep!" replied my cousin. "He's a heap safer than you are!"

I feel sad for farmers. Potato bugs ruin potato crops, and corn borers destroy corn. Pity those poor dairy farmers with butterflies everywhere.

My cousin's wife called the druggist and ordered some powerful medicine for her husband and her horse.

"Be sure and write plain on them labels which is for the horse and which is for my husband," she instructed. "I don't want nothin' to happen to that horse before spring plowin'."

Once my country cousin came to visit me in the city. He was fascinated by the paved streets. Digging his heel into the hard surface he said, "Can't blame you folks for building a town here. This ground sure ain't fittin' to plow!"

Finances

Some say that no person should keep too much to oneself. The IRS is of the same opinion.

A balanced budget is when the earning power catches up to the yearning capacity.

This is the land of plenty—everything here costs plenty.

Dr. Sawbones confronted Mrs. Hypochondriac about the bills she hadn't been paying.

"I'm very sorry about this," the doctor tried to explain, "but I don't see how I can continue to treat you because your bill is much more than it should be."

"Well, I'm certainly glad you have come to your senses, doctor," she cried. "Now, if you'll just make your bill out for what it should be, I'll write you a check!"

Stock Market Advice: It's not the bulls and bears you have to watch out for—it's the bum steers.

In modern finance things are touch and go. First they touch you for the money, then you wonder where it goes.

Money may not buy happiness, but long-term leases are available.

"My doctor vowed that he would have me walking in three months," said George.

"And did he succeed?" inquired a friend.

"You bet he did!" answered George. "With what he charged me, I had to sell my car!"

Money still talks, but you have to increase the volume if you want to get the message through.

When my son was in college he sent me this letter:

Dear Dad,

Gue$$ what I need mo$t of all? That'$ right. $end it along.

> Be$t wi$he$, Your $on,
> Ru$$.

I replied:

Dear Russ,

I'm glad to kNOw that you are NOt doing badly in college. NOthing pleases me more.

Write aNOther letter soon. As I have NO news, I must close NOw.
>Dad.

It takes a long time to pay for a new car. The other day I saw an ad that read: "For Sale: '29 Model A Ford. Take over payments."

A door-to-door salesman said to my wife, "Let me show you something your neighbor said you couldn't afford."

The old woman who lived in a shoe now has a lot of descendants who are living on a shoestring.

Remember that sales talk is trade wind.

The futility of riches is plainly stated in the Bible and the income tax form.

Income tax is Uncle Sam's version of "Truth or Consequences."

The tax office in the little town had a sign over the door as you entered that read: "Watch Your Step."
>As you left, the back of the same sign read: "Watch Your Language."

The difference between the short and long income tax forms is simple. If you use the short form, the government gets your money. If you use the long form, the accountant gets your money.

Gardening

QUESTION: What do you learn when buying a load of topsoil?

ANSWER: That while some things are dirt cheap, dirt is not one of them.

A man stopped by to see an old couple he hadn't visited in a long time. "How's John?" he asked the woman.

"Oh," she explained, "didn't you know he's dead? He went down to the garden to pull a cabbage for dinner. When he bent down, he fell dead, right there on the spot."

"That's terrible," the visitor replied. "What on earth did you do?"

"Well, what *could* I do?" the old woman answered. "I had to open a can of peas!"

My uncle Al doesn't know much about plants. Once a neighbor was showing him through her new greenhouse.

"This plant belongs to the begonia family," she explained.

"Oh," gushed my uncle, "how nice of you to look after it while they're away!"

To cultivate a garden takes
too much time and labor;
I'd rather live next door to one
and cultivate my neighbor.

My grandfather was a farmer. He didn't claim to know much, but he always had a good crop. Once a student from the state agricultural college came out.

"Your methods of cultivation are hopelessly out of date," the young man said. "Why, I'd be surprised if you get ten pounds of apples off that tree."

"So would I," my grandfather responded. "It's a pear tree!"

Farming helps a farmer remember dates. Once a census taker asked a farmer the birthdate of his daughter.

"Well," he drawled, "she was born 'bout 'tater time, but I'll be hanged if I can remember if it was diggin' or plantin' time!"

My aunt (whose elevator doesn't go all the way to the top), wrote the Agriculture Department a letter:

Dear Sirs:

Could you send me a booklet explaining

the use of different poisons for vegetables in the garden? I have lost my husband, and I have lots of different poisons on hand.

Gossip

A little girl in Sunday School proudly quoted the memory verse: "Go ye into all the world and preach the gossip."

A neighbor in our area said to her friend next door, "You know, I wouldn't say anything about Rosy unless it was good—and, oh boy, is this good!"

Her motto is: "If you can't say anything good about a person, let's hear it."

Gossip results when we throw our jaw in gear before our brain turns over. We forget that our tongue is in a wet place and likely to slip.

Have you noticed that a person usually leads with his chin when his mouth is wide open? And isn't it strange how often small talk comes in large doses.

When some folks hold a conversation, they forget to turn it loose. Some will never learn that the best way to save face is to stop shooting it off. Their idea of keeping a secret is refusing to tell who told it to them.

Two things are really bad for the heart—running up stairs and down people.

Some folks don't have much to say, but you have to listen a long time to find it out. Blessed are they who have nothing to say—and cannot be persuaded to say it.

> *I'm careful of the words I say,*
> *I keep them soft and sweet.*
> *I never know from day to day*
> *Which ones I'll have to eat.*

Out of the mouths of babes will come words they should never have heard us say in the first place.

Many friends are like a team of horses—parted by a tongue.

We have to be really careful with half-truths; we will likely repeat the wrong half.

A gossip is a person with a sense of rumor—and that's as hard to unspread as butter.

Grandchildren and Grandparents

Satisfied Grandmother: If she had it to do all over again, she would bypass children and just have grandchildren.

Her grandchild was a teenager before she actually met him. They hugged and kissed and the teenager said, "So you're my grandmother?"

"Yes," she replied, "I'm your grandmother on your father's side."

The teenager replied, "Well, I can tell you right now—you're on the wrong side!"

The proud grandfather was driving his granddaughter through the countryside pointing out agricultural points of interest.

He pointed to a herd of cattle. "Aren't those beautiful?" he asked.

"Yes, Paw-paw," said his granddaughter. "What kind of cows are those?"

"Jersey cows," explained the grandfather.

"How can you tell?" the granddaughter asked. "They're not wearing any license plates!"

QUESTION: Why did God plan for grandparents never to have babies?

ANSWER: Because they might lay a baby down and forget where they put it.

GRANDFATHER: "Is there anything worse than being old and bent?"

COLLEGE GRANDSON: "Yes, being young and broke!"

GRANDFATHER ON AIRPLANE: "Have I told you about my grandchildren?"

OCCUPANT IN THE NEXT SEAT: "No, and I certainly do appreciate it!"

An old doctor was turning his practice over to his grandson, fresh out of medical school. After a couple weeks of vacation, the old doctor returned to hear what the younger doctor thought was good news.

"Guess what, Grandad," he exclaimed. "Do you remember Mrs. Williams who has been coming to you for indigestion for thirty years? While you were gone, I prescribed some medicine and she has been cured."

The older doctor moaned, "Son, that indigestion put you through college and medical school!"

There's nothing more affectionate than grandchildren with sticky hands. And they leave a trail wherever they go. As someone put it:

> *Our rugs and floors give evidence,*
> *Enough to wear our patience thin,*
> *That one small boy with two small feet*
> *Can bring so much of the outdoors in!*

A baby has a way of making a man out of his father and a boy out of his grandfather.

Grandchildren are God's reward for growing older.

> *In spite of all their messin',*
> *Grandchildren are a blessin'.*

Health

If hospitals are places to get well, why do they serve that food?

Minor Operation: Any operation that someone else has.

NURSE: "Doctor, how was the operation?"
DOCTOR: "Just fine, but I just barely performed it in time!"
NURSE: "Was he in danger of dying?"
DOCTOR: "No, but in another two hours the patient would have recovered without it!"

Two foreign doctors performed a female operation on a grouchy woman. Afterward, one told her husband, "You vife iz now impregnable."

"Oh, yes," commented the other doctor. "No question but vot she iz now inconceivable."

"I think what you both mean to say," replied her husband, "is that she is unbearable!"

DOCTOR: "You have nothing to worry about! You'll live to be eighty."
PATIENT: "I am eighty."
DOCTOR: "What did I tell you?"

Jack Benny once responded to an extravagant round of applause with the quip: "I don't deserve this, but then I have arthritis, and I don't think I deserve that either!"

I had to quit taking tranquilizers. I realized I was being nice to people I didn't even like.

Hearing

He finally invested in a hearing aid after becoming virtually deaf. It was one of the invisible kinds.

"Well, how do you like your new hearing aid?" asked his doctor.

"I like it great. I've heard sounds in the last few weeks that I didn't know existed."

"Well, how does your family like your hearing aid?"

"Oh, nobody in my family knows I have it yet. Am I having a great time! I've changed my will three times in the last two weeks!"

WIFE: "My ear rings all the time and you don't seem to care about it."
HUSBAND: "Oh, I do care about it."
WIFE: "Well then, what do you suggest I do?"
HUSBAND: "Get an unlisted ear!"

A man and his wife both had hearing problems. "Look," he said, "when I say something to you, for goodness sake, show me that you heard me. Just grunt, say 'OK,' 'Drop dead,' 'I don't agree with you,' or just tell me that you heard me some way or another."

Her reply was rather unusual—"OK, I'll tell you when I don't hear you."

They'd lived together for sixty years, and he had never forgotten her birthday. However, as he was reading the morning newspaper over that extra cup of coffee, he noticed the date on the newspaper and remembered, "This is her birthday!"

He looked across the table to see if she had remembered. Evidently, she had forgotten too. Sitting there for the next few minutes, their sixty years together passed through his mind. What a fine wife she had been through those many years of heartaches, struggles, joys, and victories. In his mind, she was as sweet and lovely as she was on their wedding day. The only difference was that she had become a little hard of hearing over the years.

He leaned in her direction over his cup of coffee and yelled, "Wife, I'm proud of you!"

She sat straight up in her chair. Her eyes danced as she yelled, "That's nothing! I'm tired of you too!"

Heaven and Hell

One Sunday our church bulletin announced that a sermon entitled, "There Is a Hell" was to be preached at an evangelistic conference. Then it added, "Some of our leaders will be there and bring back a firsthand report."

A salesman selling medical supplies dropped by the doctor's office one scorching hot afternoon and greeted the nurse. "And how is Doc standing the heat?" he inquired.

"We don't really know," she stammered. "He's only been dead three days!"

A minister was visiting one of his ninety-year-old parishioners. "Soon," she said, "I'll be rocking in the bosom of Moses."

"No, dear," said the pastor. "The Bible says it's the bosom of Abraham."

"Well, at my age," she replied, "you don't really care much about whose bosom it is!"

The ninety-two-year-old woman at a nursing home received a visit from one of her fellow church members. "How are you feeling?" the visitor asked.

"Oh," said the lady, "I'm just worried sick!"

"What are you worried about, dear?" her friend asked. "You look like you're in good health. They are taking care of you, aren't they?"

"Yes, they are taking good care of me."

"Are you in any pain?" she asked sympathetically.

"No, I have never had a pain in my life."

"Well, what are you worried about?" her friend queried.

She leaned back in her chair and slowly explained her major worry. "Every close friend I ever had has already died and gone on to heaven. I'm afraid they're all wondering where I went."

A sign on a bulletin board of a church down the street announced the topic for Sunday's sermon: "Do You Know What Hell Is?"

Underneath, someone had scribbled, "Come and hear our organist!"

Holidays

During college days our neighbor in a next-door apartment gave their small boy a toy drum for Christmas. The kid beat on the contraption day and night. Finally, I grew weary of it. I gave the lad a new pocketknife and asked him if he knew what was inside the drum.

Santa's helpers are only subordinate clauses.

At Christmastime the Sunday School teacher rehearsed the boys for a play that was to be presented to the church during the worship hour. Four children, carrying huge, cut-out letters, were lined up to spell "S-T-A-R."

When the program began the audience began to chuckle. The four little performers marched out on the platform—in reverse order!

Husbands and Wives

My wife and I got married for better or worse.
I couldn't do better and she couldn't do worse.

A husband who brags that he never made a mistake has a wife who made a big one!

My secret to a long, happy married life is simple. I try to treat my wife in such a way that if I died, it would take more than a hot water bottle to replace me.

Frankly, marriage is like twirling a baton, turning handsprings, or eating with chopsticks. It looks easy until you try it.

On our fortieth wedding anniversary my wife said warmly and affectionately, "Will you love me when I'm old and gray?"

"Well, of course," I assured her. "Haven't I loved you through four other colors?"

Before I married Shirley, dear,
I was her pumpkin pie,
Her precious peach, her honey lamb,
The apple of her eye.
But after years of married life,

This thought I pause to utter;
Those fancy names are gone, and now
I'm just her bread and butter.
My wife does not wish for jewels or furs
Or lovely serenades at dawn.
She only wishes that I would put
The toothpaste cap back on!

Give my wife an inch—and the whole family goes on a diet.

I heard my wife telling the neighbor that I was a model husband. I felt pretty good until I looked up the word in the dictionary: "A model is a small imitation of the real thing."

Husbands and wives need each other, but often find difficulty getting along. They've been likened to porcupines on a cold, winter night–the trick is staying close enough together to keep from freezing to death, and far enough apart to keep from sticking each other to death.

They are much like the swimming instructor who asked a little boy to explain the buddy system.

"It's somebody you drown with," he answered.

Insurance

SUPERVISOR TO AGENT: "I noticed here that you have written an insurance policy for a man who is ninety-five years of age."

INSURANCE AGENT: "Yes. What a tremendous deal!"

SUPERVISOR: "What do you mean 'tremendous deal'? Do you realize how old that man is?"

AGENT: "Yes, I realize how old he is. I checked the census reports. Do you realize how *few* people die after the age of ninety-five?"

The following are actual statements found on insurance forms where car drivers attempted to summarize the details of an accident in the fewest words possible:

"Coming home, I drove into the wrong house and collided with a tree I don't have."

"The other car collided with mine without giving warning of its intentions."

"I thought my window was down, but I found out it was up when I put my head through it."

"I collided with a stationary truck coming the other way."

"A truck backed through my windshield into my wife's face."

"A pedestrian hit me and went under my car."

"The pedestrian had no idea which direction to run, so I ran over him."

"I saw a slow-moving, sad-faced old gentleman as he bounced off the roof of my car."

"The indirect cause of the accident was a little guy in a small car with a big mouth."

"I was thrown from my car as it left the road. I was later found in a ditch by some stray cows."

"The telephone pole was approaching. I was attempting to swerve out of its way when I struck the front end."

The insurance agent was surprised to find a couple in a retirement village with no insurance. In his effort to sell a policy to the husband, he said, "How in the world would your wife carry on if you should die!"

"Well," answered the husband, "I really don't care how she carries on after I die, just as long as she behaves herself as long as I'm alive."

Memories

Times sure have changed. Today school systems spend a fortune soundproofing rooms with special kinds of expensive floors and ceilings. When I was a boy, schools soundproofed me.

I was born at a very early age, at home, so I could be near my mother. I don't want to say I was an ugly baby, but the doctor took one look at me and made a citizen's arrest of my father.

I was six months old before I saw the light of day. My mother was nearsighted and kept diapering the wrong end.

There were six kids in all. One day a stranger stopped my mother and asked, "Lady, are all those your kids, or are you on a picnic?"

"Mister," my mother sighed, "they're all mine, and believe me, it's no picnic."

Some folks had six rooms and a bath. We had four rooms and a path. It was what you might call a deep-seated tradition.

One of our neighbors, a farmer down the road, was rather prolific. He had ten kids. During the fall season he took them to the fair to see a prize bull.

Approaching the ticket seller, the farmer said, "Mister, this here's my wife and ten kids. I'll give you five dollars to let us take a look at that bull."

The ticket seller, looking at him and then the ten kids, scratched his head. "Tell you what," he said, "I'll give you ten dollars if you'll let me go get that bull and let him take a look at you!"

My country cousin, Tom, went off to one of those big-city colleges. After he graduated he returned to work on his dad's farm. He plowed the same; but when he got to the end of a row, instead of saying, "Whoa, hew, and gee," he said, "Halt, Rebecca, pivot and proceed!"

For Christmas dinner we always had plenty of chicken and dressing. My little sister said, "I don't like the chicken, but I like the bread he ate!"

I'll never forget the day I graduated from grammar school—I was so nervous I could hardly shave.

I was always getting in trouble at school for things I didn't do—like arithmetic, history, biology, and so forth.

The teachers kept asking me hard questions, like one asked me to define space.

"I can't put it into words," I replied, "but I have it in my head."

Memory

You're getting old when there's no question in your mind that there's no question in your mind.

Two elderly ladies were sitting on a porch rocking back and forth in rocking chairs. "Sally," said one, "do you ever think about the hereafter?"

As quick as a flash, Sally replied, "All the time! I go into a room and look around and say, 'Now what was it I came in here after?'"

"Who Wrote Whom?"

Just a line to say I'm living,
that I'm not among the dead.
Though I'm getting more forgetful
and mixed up in the head.
I got used to my arthritis,
to my dentures I'm resigned.
I can manage my bifocals,
but I sure do miss my mind.
For sometimes I can't remember
when I stand at the foot of the stairs,
If I must go up for something,
or have I just come down from there.
And before the fridge so often,

my poor mind is filled with doubt,
Have I just put food away,
or have I come to take some out?
And there's time when it is dark
with my nightcap on my head,
I don't know if I'm retiring,
or just getting out of bed.
So, if it's my turn to write you,
there's no need for getting sore,
I may think that I have written,
and don't want to be a bore.
So, remember that I love you,
and wish that you were near.
But now it's nearly mail time
so I must say good-bye, dear.
There I stand before the mailbox,
with a face so very red.
Instead of mailing you my letter,
I had opened it instead.

—Anonymous

OLDER PATIENT: "Doc, I think I am becoming forgetful."
DOCTOR: "Sorry to hear that."
PATIENT: "What do you suggest I do, Doc?"
DOCTOR: "Pay me in advance!"

I recently met a Texan with a bad case of amnesia—he couldn't remember the Alamo!

Mottoes

John D. Yeck is the founder of an organization that he calls, "The Let's Have Better Mottoes Association, Inc." Some of his funniest mottoes shared in his monthly newsletter are as follows:

Fools rush in where fools have been before.

I'm so completely open-minded on the issue that I'll even listen to your fantastically stupid, idiotic opinion.

To avoid duplication, make three copies.

Do not disturb—Genius at werk.

It's called "take-home pay" because you can't afford to go anywhere else with it.

Success is relative; the greater the success, the more relatives.

My work is so secret even I don't know what I'm doing.

Anyone can be a winner—unless, of course, there's a second entry.

It's better to have loafed and lost than never to have loafed at all.

The slower you work, the fewer misteaks you make.

People claim I'm indecisive but I'm not so sure.

Experience is what tells you you've made a mistake . . . again.

I am not arbitrary, and I won't discuss it further.

I'm going to become more assertive if it's 100 percent OK with you.

Please don't argue. I've changed my mind already.

Worry kills more people than work because more people worry than work.

I never make a mistake, but I'm getting tired of doing nothing.

I respect your opinion, but I'd respect it even more if you'd keep it to yourself.

If at first you don't succeed, look in the wastebasket for the directions.

Procrastination avoids boredom—there's always something left to do.

For every vision there is an equal and opposite revision.

If Murphy's Law can go wrong, IT WILL.

You can say anything you please around here but some things only once.

If at first you succeed, try to hide your astonishment.

You must have learned from others' mistakes. You haven't had time to think all those up yourself.

Your visit is the highlight of my day; so you know what kind of day I've had.

If you look like your passport picture, you probably need the trip.

Pets

Did you hear about the hummingbird and doorbell that fell in love, got married, and had a little humdinger?

Our neighbor looked out the front window and saw her small son coming up the walk carrying a little spotted puppy. She met him at the door and commanded, "You take that puppy right back where you got him and bring your baby sister home!"

Did you hear about the little boy who practiced his violin. As he scratched away on the instrument the hound dog howled dismally along with the boy's playing.

Finally, in desperation, his mother screamed at her son, "I can't stand it anymore! Can't you play something the dog doesn't know!"

A man and his wife were planning a vacation in Florida. They didn't know what to do with their dog, so the husband wrote the hotel manager and asked if dogs were allowed. He promptly answered:

Dear Sir:

I've been in the hotel business for thirty years and I've never had to call the police to eject a disorderly dog; never had a dog set fire to a bed with a cigarette; never found a hotel towel in a dog's suitcase; and never had a dog leave a glass ring on the top of the dresser. Your dog is welcome.

Signed: the Manager

P.S. If your dog will vouch for you, you can come along too.

Politics

If the world keeps getting smaller, how come it costs more to run it?

If the country is going to the dogs, maybe it's because the congressmen haven't been to obedience school.

He took his Social Security check down to the bank to deposit it. As he stood and waited in the long line, he inadvertently began to nervously fold and unfold his check.

Finally his turn came at the teller's window. As he handed the teller a ruffled government check she said, "Sir, can't you read this check? It says, 'Do not fold, spindle, or mutilate.'"

"So?" replied the customer.

"Well," said the teller, "You shouldn't do that. The government doesn't like it."

Looking her straight in the eye he replied, "Well, the government does a lot of things I don't like too!"

Two residents of a retirement village were discussing the two candidates for mayor of the city. "The only good thing about it," said one, "is that only one of them will be elected."

A local politician was visiting a nursing home. "Well," one little old lady replied to the persistent politician, "you're my second choice."

"Oh, I'm honored by that, madam, but may I ask, who is your first choice?"

"Oh," she replied casually, "anybody else who is running for the same office!"

An election year is when the air is filled with speeches and vice versa.

I listened to one of those politicians waxing eloquent one day.

"If I'm elected," he promised, "I'll get rid of socialism, communism, and anarchism."

"Yeah," interrupted an old man from the back of the room, "and let's throw out rheumatism too!"

The reason so many politicians are anxious to get reelected is they are afraid to try to make a living back home under the laws they passed in Washington.

Have you noticed that politicians' promises of yesterday are the taxes of today?

Some politicians' minds are like concrete—thoroughly mixed and permanently set.

Recreation

Nothing increases your golf score like a witness.

My doctor gives me lots of advice. Recently he said, "The best thing for you is to give up golf, tennis, and keep earlier hours."

"Aw, Doc," I replied, "I don't deserve the best. What's second best?"

The recreation director for a certain retirement village decided to revive some of the dances of the olden days.

It was "Twist" night and the senior adults were "cutting the rug." Two dogs walked by the recreation room and looked in. One said, "What in the world are they doing in there?"

The other dog said, "I don't know, but if we did it they would medicate us!"

Old fishermen never die—they just smell that way!

The fisherman watched a weatherbeaten old guide in the adjoining boat carefully cut a fishing line partway through a few inches above the brightly colored lure.

"Why are you doing that?" he asked.

"I'm fixing to take an amateur out pretty soon," the old fisherman explained. "He'll likely snag a fair-sized fish right off. When he goes to lift him into the boat the line will break. That feller will tell all his friends about the big one that got away." The old man looked about slyly, then added, "What's more, he'll come back here every summer for the rest of his life trying to catch that big one."

On fishing trips we never face famine. We always take along a can of salmon.

On a fishing trip I was outfitted in complete fishing regalia, including a hat with my fishing license prominently displayed on its side.

After fishing all day with no luck, my son said to me, "Dad, why don't you turn your hat around so the fish can see your license?"

Remarriage

Ben and Mary had lived together as a married couple for more than sixty years. On one occasion she went to her beautician with this request, "Make me look like Ben's second wife."

One couple was so old when they married that they applied to Medicare for payments on their honeymoon.

The groundskeeper at the cemetery heard the cries of an elderly man as he lay across a grave. He was crying, "Why did you die, oh, why did you die?"

"Was that your wife?" he asked.

"No, no, it wasn't my wife. Oh, why did you die? Why did you die?"

"Was it a friend of yours?"

"No, no, I never knew the person. Oh, why did you die? Why did you die?"

"It was not a member of your family?"

"No, it was not a member of my family. Oh, why did you die? Why did you die?"

"Then who, sir, is buried in that grave?"

"My wife's first husband."

The older man knelt before his new and exciting love. "I have two questions to ask you," he said.

"Yes, yes," was the enthusiastic response.

"Will you marry me?"

"Oh, yes. I was waiting for you to ask me! Now what is your second question?"

"Will you help me up?"

My bachelor neighbor sneaked up behind an older woman, covered her eyes with his hands, and said, "I'm going to kiss you if you can't tell me who I am in three guesses."

"George Washington! Thomas Jefferson! Abraham Lincoln!" she answered quickly.

I should have known better when I proposed to her and asked, "Darling, do you think you can live on what I make?"

"Sure," she replied, "but I don't know what you're going to live on."

Retirement

The worst thing about retirement is having to drink coffee on your own time.

We could all retire comfortably if we could sell our experience for what it cost us.

A young preacher was serving as a volunteer chaplain at a large nursing home. He had never performed a wedding, so he asked an older preacher in town what to do in case he forgot during the wedding ceremony. He was advised, "Just quote Scripture until something comes to you."

Soon the young preacher was called upon to perform the wedding ceremony for a widow and widower in the nursing home. Sure enough, right in the middle of the ceremony he forgot what to say next. So, thinking of the advice of the older preacher, he started quoting Scripture. But the only Scripture he could remember was, "Father, forgive them for they know not what they do!"

FIRST WIDOW: "They say he married her because her first husband left her a million dollars."

SECOND WIDOW: "Oh, I don't think he's that kind of a fellow. I think he would have married her regardless of who left her the million dollars."

Two men were discussing the hobbies and crafts offered at the retirement village in which they and their wives were living. "Is your wife an active member of the sewing circle?" asked one man.

"No," the other man shook his head, "she just sits there and sews!"

Several years after his retirement, Joe decided to go back to the office and see how things were going. Just to see how well he was remembered, he decided to go in and ask for himself.

"Can I speak to Joe Smith?" he asked a bright young secretary in the front office.

"Oh," she said, "Joe Smith doesn't work here anymore."

"Well," he said, "let me speak to the man who filled his vacancy."

"Well," the secretary said, "Joe didn't leave a vacancy!"

speaking

Oratory is the art of making sounds deep within the chest sound like important messages from the heart.

I was a promising speaker in college—they made me promise never to try it again.

I almost quit speaking on account of my throat—audiences kept threatening to cut it!

Actually, at my last speaking engagement I drew a line three blocks long. Then some smart aleck took my chalk away from me!

I know I don't have any talent for speaking; but now I've become so famous at it, I can't give it up.

I always start speaking at 7 P.M. sharp and end at 8 P.M. dull.

Not long ago at a speaking engagement, I noticed a sign near the speaker's platform (for the benefit of people taking flash pictures) that read:

"Do not photograph the speaker while he is addressing the audience. Shoot him as he leaves the platform."

Once I was hurrying to the auditorium to make a speech when a reporter stopped me and asked me a deep philosophical question.

"Don't bother me now," I snapped, "I've got to make a speech and this is no time to think!"

My wife is really the speaker in the family. She speaks 150 words a minute with gusts up to 180.

She believes in the discipline of silence and can talk hours about it.

That's why they call it the "mother tongue"— the father seldom gets to use it.

One of my kinfolk donated a loudspeaker to our church in memory of his wife.

Special Occasions

They had lived together in the backwoods for over fifty years. To celebrate their fiftieth anniversary, he took her to a large city and they checked into a plush hotel.

She said to the bellman, "We refuse to settle for such a small room. No windows, no bed, no fan," she complained.

"But, madam!"

"Don't 'But, madam' me," she continued. "You can't treat us like we're a couple of fools just because we don't travel much, and we've never been to the big city, and never spent the night at a hotel. I'm going to complain to the manager."

"Madam," the bellman said, "this isn't your room; this is the elevator!"

The nicest gift is always something you made yourself . . . like money.

She was ninety years of age. Her little house was filled with knick-knacks and whatnots people had given her for her birthday.

A friend asked, "And what do you want for your ninetieth birthday?"

"Give me a kiss," she answered, "so I won't have to dust it!"

You will always stay young if you live honestly, sleep sufficiently, eat slowly, work industriously, and fib about your age.

My wife refuses to have candles on her birthday cake. She said she was in no mood to make light of her age.

It's just as well. If we put all those candles on the cake it would be a fire hazard.

Sports

A five-year-old girl had gone fishing with her grandfather. After an hour or so her grandfather asked her, "Are you having any luck?"

She replied indignantly, "No, I don't think my worm is really trying."

At every ball game there are a few men who can play every position superbly without an error. Now if we can just get them to put down their hot dogs and climb down from the bleachers.

My wife complains about my playing golf.

"You never think of anything but golf," she declared. "Why, I'll bet you don't even remember the day we got married."

"Of course, I do, honey," I insisted. "It was the day I sank that forty-foot putt."

Overheard in the clubhouse of a retirement village: "It's not that I cheat," the golfer explained, "it's just that I play golf for my health, and a low score makes me feel better!"

The best golfer at a retirement village was an eighty-year-old man. He could hit the ball

250 yards every time. However, he was losing his eyesight and couldn't follow the trajectory of his ball.

He met another eighty-year-old friend who was not as good a golfer but had 20/20 vision. "I have a great idea," he exclaimed. "Let's play golf together. You can see well enough to tell where my ball lands."

On their first day out, the first man stepped up to the ball and hit it 275 yards. The other man replied, "I see it, I see it, I see it."

"Where did it go?" asked the long hitter.

The other man turned to him with a blank stare and said, "I forgot!"

I like to go to football games, but they always seat me between the hot dog peddler and his best customer. Or they place me beside a silly spectator who thinks he's got four quarters in which to finish a fifth.

Once our boys' team played a girls' team in football. I don't know what the score was; but when the game was over, our team had been penalized a mile behind the goal line for holding.

Golfers say they shoot their age. It's more like their weight, if you ask me.

It doesn't seem fair. By the time a person can afford to lose a golf ball, he can't hit it that far.

Golf is a lot like taxes—you drive hard to get to the green and then wind up in the hole.

Success

Old Age: Just when you're successful enough to
sleep late, you're so old you always wake
up early.

The secret of success is to always have more
answers than people have questions.

The Bible teaches us importunity—to keep
on asking. My little daughter came here
already knowing that. One long, tiring day my
wife and I finally got her to bed, said our
prayers, tucked her in, turned off the lights,
and retreated to the family room to watch
some uninterrupted television.

Hardly had we settled down when we
heard our small daughter's voice cry, "Daddy!
I want a drink of water."

"You've had a drink of water," I replied.
"Now, go to sleep."

After a couple of minutes again came the
plaintive plea, "Daddy! I need a drink of
water."

"No!" I said in a stern voice, "and if you
ask me one more time, I'll come in there and
spank you."

A brief silence followed. Then her wee voice wailed, "Daddy, when you come in here to spank me, would you bring me a drink of water?"

Besides, success is something that always comes faster to the man your wife almost married.

When you make your mark in the world, somebody will come along with an eraser.

If you're going to climb higher, you've got to grab the branches, not the blossoms.

There's plenty of room at the top, but there's no room to sit down.

The world isn't interested in the storm you encountered, but only if you brought in the ship.

Isn't it strange that people who are successful and have what they want are fond of telling unsuccessful people who don't have what they want that they really don't want it.

Survival

"To the Class of '42"

Attention, 1942 classmates! We are survivors!

It is said that man has three ages: (1) youth, (2) middle, and (3) "You haven't changed a bit!" But change is the name of the game.

Consider: We were before television, before penicillin, before polio shots, frozen foods, Xerox, contact lenses, Frisbees, and the Pill. We were before radar, credit cards, split atoms, laser beams, and ballpoint pens. We were before pantyhose, dishwashers, clothes dryers, electric blankets, and automatic shift. We got married first and then lived together. How quaint can you be!

In our time, closets were for clothes, not for "coming out of." Bunnies were small rabbits and rabbits were not Volkswagens. We thought a deep cleavage was something a butcher did. Designer jeans were scheming girls named Jean or Jeanne, and having a meaningful relationship meant getting along well with your cousin. We thought fast food was what you ate during Lent, and outer space was the balcony at the local theater. We were before househusbands, gay rights, computer dating, dual careers, and commuter marriages. We were before day-care centers, group therapy, and nursing homes. We never heard of FM radio, computer chips, tape decks, electric typewriters, artificial hearts, word processors, yogurt, and guys wearing earrings.

We hit the scene when there were 5-and-10-cent stores where you bought things for five and ten cents. The ice-cream store sold ice-cream cones for a nickel or a dime. For one nickel you could make a phone call, buy a Coke, or enough stamps to mail one letter and two postcards. You could buy a new Chevy coupe for $590, but who could afford one? And a pity, too, because gas was only ten cents a gallon!

In our day cigarette smoking was fashionable, grass was mowed, Coke was a cold drink at the corner drug store, and pot was something you cooked in. Break dancing was something Charlie Henderson played for in the gym at the lunch period. Rock music was a Grandma's lullaby, and aids were helpers in the cafeteria.

We were certainly not before the difference between the sexes was discovered, but we were surely before the sex change. We made do with what we had. And we were the last generation that was so dumb as to think you needed a husband to have a baby.

But . . . we survived!

—Anonymous

Television

The difference between watching television and dying is that with television, other people's lives flash before your eyes.

The television salesman gave a man and his wife a demonstration of how to use a remote controlled set. He hooked it up in their living room, took the remote control transmitter a block down the street, and switched channels without difficulty.

But the wife didn't like it. She got tired of walking a block away every time she wanted to change channels.

Who said opportunity only knocks once? Television is giving us a second chance to see old movies we couldn't afford to see twenty years ago.

Television is called a medium because so much of it is neither rare nor well done. Sometimes television programs are so bad I'm tempted to dredge the channel.

Television has increased the cost of living. When I was a boy I could see a western for twenty-five cents. Today it costs three hundred dollars for a VCR to watch the same western.

I really don't mind my wife serving TV dinners, but here lately she's started serving reruns in the summer.

Some folks think television advertising is new. Not so. It's actually the same form of selling that was common in the patent medicine shows of the past.

The medicine man would put a couple of song-and-dance people on a platform and when a crowd gathered, he came out and sold his snake oil.

Television has only upgraded the song-and-dance people and increased the cost of the snake oil.

Time

By the time you finally stop and smell the roses, somebody's just spread out the fertilizer.

My doctor once mentioned that he rarely attended a patient's funeral.

"Of course not," my wife chattered. "If you tried, it wouldn't leave you time for anything else."

> *When guests have declared they*
> *must be going,*
> *And my vision is getting blurry,*
> *Why do I say (to my own dismay)*
> *So convincingly,*
> *"What's your hurry?"*

My wife is the world's worst at getting instructions mixed up. For instance, when we were married, she bought one of those fancy, electric coffeemakers. It had all kinds of gadgets on it.

The salesman carefully explained how the timer worked. "You plug it in, set the timer, and go back to bed. When you get up, the coffee is ready."

A couple of weeks later my wife was back in the store, and the salesman asked her how she liked her new coffeemaker.

"Great!" she replied, "But there's one thing I don't understand. Why do I have to go to bed every time I want to make a pot of coffee?"

Travel

He was up in years before he ever had the opportunity to go to an airport. He had never seen an escalator. He stood in amazement watching the escalator go up and come down. Then, he noticed a whole busload of ladies from a local retirement village get on the escalator going down.

As he stood there watching the escalator come back up, it was filled with a group of young college coeds coming home for the holidays.

He said to himself, *I'm going to go home right now and get Ma and put her on this machine!*

A group of ladies from a retirement village loaded onto the bus to observe a local art exhibit. The artist himself was present to explain his paintings.

One lady walked up to an abstract painting and asked the artist, "What in the world is that supposed to be?"

The artist said condescendingly, "Well, my dear lady, that's supposed to be a mother and her child."

"Well, why isn't it?" asked the art critic.

A plane full of retirees headed for Florida was gripped with fear when the pilot announced, "Two of our engines are on fire; we are flying through a heavy fog, and it has eliminated all our visibility."

The passengers were numb with fear, except for one—a retired minister. "Now, now, keep calm," he said. "Let's all bow our heads and pray."

Immediately they bowed their heads to pray—except one man. "Why aren't you bowing your head to pray?" the minister asked.

"I don't know how to pray," replied the passenger.

"Well, just do something religious!" instructed the minister.

The man got up and passed his hat down the aisle, taking an offering.

Remember riding in a car in the thirties and forties reading the Burma Shave signs? The jingles on successive signs were a delight.

> Within this vale
> of toil and sin
> Your head grows bald
> but not your chin.

She kissed the hairbrush
by mistake.
She thought it was
her husband Jake.

I proposed to Ida;
Ida refused.
I'da won Ida
if I'da used
Burma Shave.

They missed the turn;
Car was whizz'n.
Fault was her'n;
Funeral his'n.

Does your husband misbehave,
grunt and grumble,
pant and rave?
Shoot the brute
some Burma Shave.

Unclassified

There is one thing that most of us do better than anyone else—read our own handwriting.

Some people have their feet planted firmly on the ground . . . and others just move like it.

An eight-year-old boy wrote a composition about his father:
"He can climb the highest mountain or swim the biggest ocean. He can fly the fastest plane and fight the strongest tiger. My father can do anything. But most of the time he just carries out the garbage!"

Several years ago a friend was in trouble, and I helped him out.
"I won't forget you," he promised. He didn't. He's in trouble again, and he just called me.

Our house is a bungalow—the carpenters bungled the job, and we still owe for it.

I read in the newspaper about a man in Connecticut who was arrested for stealing a chicken from a market. He claimed the chicken flew under his coat. But the police doubted his story since the chicken was frozen.

The other day a young girl rang the doorbell and tried to sell me a ticket to a band concert.

"Sorry," I quickly replied, "I can't make it, but my spirit will be there with you."

"Good!" she replied. "I have two-dollar, three-dollar, and five-dollar tickets. Where would your spirit like to sit?"

A little boy came home with a note from his teacher pinned to his jacket:
"Dear Parents:

"If you'll promise not to believe everything that your child tells you happens at school, I'll promise not to believe everything your child tells me happens at home."

Once a Texan visited Australia. He told the folks down under how much bigger and better things were in Texas. Suddenly a kangaroo jumped in front of him.

"What in tarnation was that?" the startled Texan asked.

"You mean you don't have grasshoppers in Texas?" an Australian calmly replied.

Vacations

Vacation: a trip that puts you in the pink—and leaves you in the red.

Sunburn: Getting what you basked for.

A man is really getting smart when he realizes that vacations are disguised shopping sprees.

A man and his wife were on vacation. In a remote area they found a little "greasy spoon" restaurant.

"We'll each have two eggs, toast, and a cup of coffee," the man said to the waitress. "And, by the way, we'd like a few kind words."

The waitress promptly brought the order to the couple and walked away.

"What about our kind words?" the man asked.

The waitress leaned over and whispered in his ear, "Don't eat those eggs!"

A friend of mine went to Florida for his health. While there, he suddenly died. His body was shipped back home for burial. As friends viewed the body, one said, "Doesn't he look wonderful!"

"Yes," replied another, "those two weeks in Florida did him a world of good."

I love taking vacation videos so I can get back and find out what a wonderful time I had.

> When vacations are over you often find,
> As you give it a backward look,
> You could have made out with
>   half the clothes,
> And twice the money you took.
> Little bankroll ere we part,
> Let me hug you to my heart;
> All the year I've clung to you—
> I've been faithful, you've been true!
> Little bankroll, in a day,
> You and I will start away
> To a good vacation spot—
> I'll come back, but you will not.

Weather

The weather is sometimes unpleasant. I remember a year that was so bad it lasted thirteen months.

Don't you just hate muggy days? Everything that's supposed to stick together comes apart, and everything that's supposed to come apart sticks together.

I can just see it now: two cavemen huddled close to their fire. Outside it's raining, sleeting, thundering, and storming. One grumbles to the other, "You know, we never had this crazy weather before they started using bows and arrows!"

Our local weatherman has a way of putting things. Last winter he reported it was "Still and clear—still snowing and clear up to your knees!"
One day he read the weather bulletin that called for fog. Looking out the window, he saw it was raining. So he added, "But the fog is presently running down the gutters!"

Many a day I've had to shovel six inches of "partly cloudy" off my walk.

Widows and Widowers

A woman brought an old picture of her dead husband, wearing a hat, to the photographer. She wanted to know if the photographer could remove the hat from the picture. He assured her he could and asked her what side of his head he parted his hair on.

"I forgot," she said. "But you can see that for yourself when you take off his hat."

Soon after her husband died, she decided it was time to learn to drive a car. On her first trip to town, she drove right through a red light. "Don't you know what that sign means?" asked an angry policeman. "It means 'Stop'!" he explained.

"Oh, I'm so sorry, Officer," the elderly widow said.

"Haven't you ever driven before?" he asked.

"Well, yes and no."

"'Yes and no.' What kind of answer is that?"

"Well, I have driven before, but this is the first time I've driven from the front seat!"

Wills

There was a large gathering in the attorney's office to hear the reading of the will. The attorney announced, "This is one of the shortest wills you've ever heard."

Then, he lifted the paper before his eyes and read, "Being of sound mind, I spent every last cent before I died!"

Two widows were visiting together in a retirement center. One said, "My husband left me well fixed. I've got enough to live on the rest of my life."

"Well," the second one remarked, "my husband didn't do too well by me. In fact, he didn't even leave any insurance."

"You seem to be pretty well off," answered the first lady.

"I got the house and several other things, and I guess I've got enough to live on the rest of my life."

The first lady noticed a large diamond on her hand and remarked, "Where did you get the money to buy that gorgeous diamond ring?" she asked.

"Well, in his will he left a thousand dollars to buy a casket and five thousand dollars to buy the stone," she replied. "This," she said, pointing to the diamond ring, "is the stone!"

It's a man's world.

When he's born, people ask, "How's the mother?"

When he marries, people ask, "What did the bride wear?"

And when he dies, they ask, "How much did he leave her?"

For years, I pretended to love my rich aunt's cats so she would remember me in her will. It worked! When she died she left me the cats.

But it was different with my rich uncle. I found his doctor and thanked him for his treatment.

"You're not a patient of mine," the doctor replied.

"I know," I explained cheerfully, "but my uncle was, and I'm his heir!"

Work

QUESTION: What's the worst part of doing nothing?
ANSWER: You can't take the day off!

All the world's a stage and nobody wants to be a stagehand.

What a great country! People come here to make an honest living, and they hardly have any competition.

Dr. Quack advised his patient that the best thing that he could do was to get back to work immediately.

"Will that help my condition?" uttered the patient.

"Well, no," answered the doctor, "but at least you'll be able to pay me!"

Isn't it strange that work is something that when we have it we wish we didn't; when we don't we wish we did; and the object of most of it is to be able to afford not to do any of it?

My neighbor is lazy. He just sits in his easy chair. If his ship ever came in, he wouldn't bother to unload it.

One woman said that her husband tried farming and gave it up because there were too many ups and downs. He had to wake up, then get up, wash up, chow down, and hitch up. Then when he checked up, he didn't have enough to pay down, so he just gave up.

Working makes me tired way up into next month. Besides, I need my beauty rest. Actually, I sleep well at nights and pretty well in the mornings, but in the afternoons I just toss and turn.

Times have changed. Forty years ago we worked twelve hours a day and it was called economic slavery. Today, we work fourteen hours a day and it's called moonlighting.

The younger generation doesn't seem to realize that getting up in the mornings is merely a matter of mind over mattress.

Worry

Psychiatrist: A man who doesn't have to worry as long as others do.

Don't worry what others may think of you. They're probably not thinking of you anyway.

"Now, Jim," said the doctor, "as I have repeatedly told you after many thorough examinations, there is absolutely nothing wrong with your heart. Please stop worrying about it. If it will make you feel any better, I will personally guarantee that your heart will last as long as you live!"

When I speak before a group, I get as nervous as a mosquito at Fort Lauderdale's beach. I know what I'm there for; I just don't know where to start.

Did you hear about the kangaroo who complained to the doctor, "I don't know what's wrong with me lately. I don't feel jumpy"?

Worry is as useless as whispering in a boiler factory.

Ulcers result from mountain climbing over molehills.

> *It's the little things that bother*
> *And put us on a rack;*
> *You can sit upon a mountain,*
> *But not upon a tack.*

Sometimes I worry at night and can't go to sleep. Somebody told me to put a wastebasket beside my bed, and when I have trouble sleeping just pretend I'm throwing my worries in it. But it didn't work. Just about the time I was falling asleep the basket would overflow and I'd have to get up and empty it!

I used to worry about what people were thinking about me. Then I realized they weren't thinking about me at all. Instead, they were worrying about what other people were thinking of them.

Wrinkles

Most people don't mind the hands of time as much as the feet of crows.

CHILDHOOD: That time of life when you make funny faces in the mirror.
MIDDLE AGE: That time of life when the mirror gets even.

All of those formulas for staying young will be totally unsuccessful until they learn how to iron out a few wrinkles.